The Archived Venue:

Inside The Lost Poetic Vault Of A Chosen Scholar (Vol. 2)

B-poet

THE ARCHIVED VENUE:
Inside The Lost Poetic Vault of a Chosen Scholar (Vol. 2)
Copyright © 2023 **B-poet**

ISBN (Paperback): 978-1-958475-13-3
ISBN (Ebook): 978-1-958475-14-0

Freelance Poetry LLC
Suite #130
5348 Vegas Drive
Las Vegas, NV 89108

Printed in the United States of America

PROMINENT
BOOKS

5830 E 2nd St, Ste 7000 #9983
Casper, WY 82609
USA

Contents

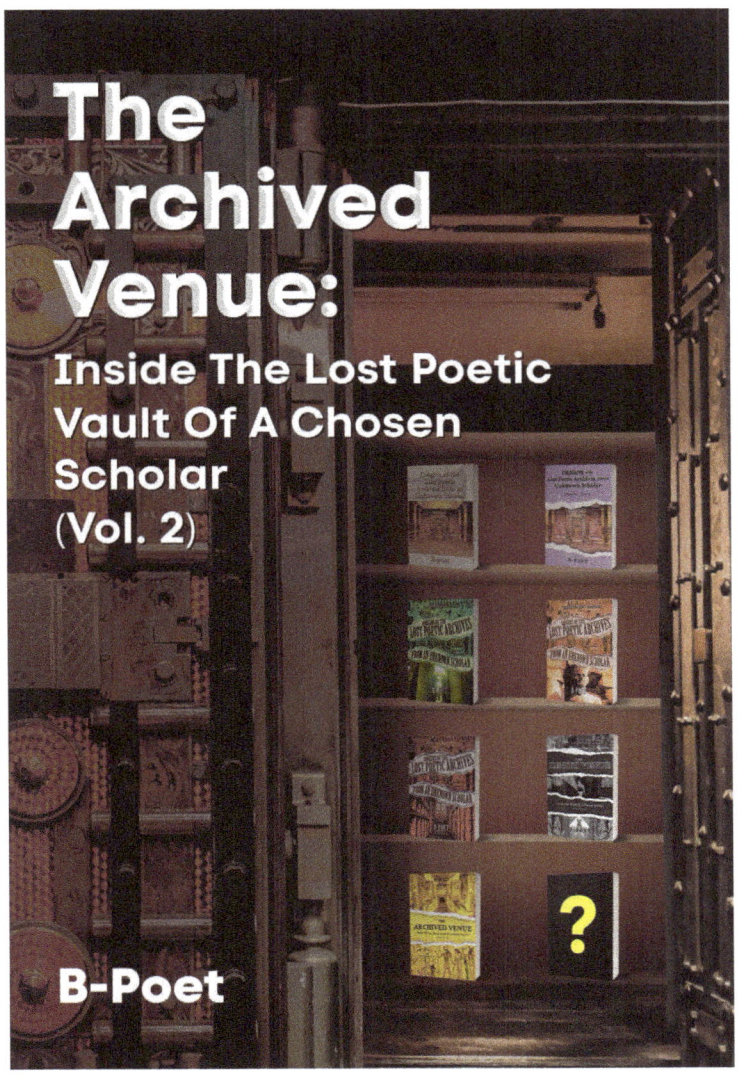

The Archived Venue:
Inside The Lost Poetic Vault Of A Chosen Scholar (Vol. 2)

B-Poet

This *Collector's Edition* will intrigue readers to
Experience the *Abounded Vaults* and B-poet's
First discovery of the *Lost Poetic Archives* as
You venture into *The Zenith Venue*
His coveted *Memoirs* are awaiting to be revealed at…

Originsofthelostpoeticarchives.godaddysites.com

Being Alone In A World Full Of People

(Version 2)

How can we still be
Quarantined *spiritually* and *socially*
With so many people
On the planet
As time runs rapid
Our personal history
As individuals
Will become evident
While the plight
For our lives
Remains an open book present
That's unfolding
Day in and *Day out*
More and *More people*
Are becoming superficial beings
For popularity reasons
Throughout the course of our present-day time
In this reality game called life

The Waiting Game

The cost of waiting
Is so high
As a moment toward attainment
Contrasted a reality nicknamed
Now and *Why*
It's hard to embrace
How a king's been
Put in his place
By a pawn
Who's already checkmated him

Since the beginning of time
The cost of losing
The Waiting Game
Remains unrivaled
So a pawn can capture
The king's bluffed royalty stature
After the king realized
Why defeat came
Ever so swiftly
To end his ruling game
Within its entirety

Disgusted From Within

Too much time has been wasted
In the blink of an eye
What could have been
Has been blown out like a candle in the wind

Where can you find the strength to persevere
Once the chance has gone
It will no longer appear
It's hard to pretend

The portrait you tried to place yourself in
Was a precious moment to capture
Where lives were changed
Since the cause of it meant more

For what it was worth
But ignorance chose to steal it
From your grasp to seize
A moment

Where everyone could have been receptive
To position themselves
At gaining a better stance for living life
Would have been their main aim

But now all we have
Is a shattered image of *me* and *everyone else*
Whose been afflicted by the *spirit of suppression, guilt, shame
Negativity*, and *The blame game*

Thus we continue to carry on like a torch with a burning flame
Not relevant enough for gaining our attention
To serve as a proper foundation for our lives
What could have been

Is the question
I'm trying to answer
Because I'm sick of living this so-called lie
Which is my life ***Disgusted From Within***

Hostility's Volcano

Erupting hot lava
From unsettled scores of revenge
At wit's end
Is the molten rock
From the bottom up
Corrupt enough to surface
Among *friends* and *enemies* alike
Who are never at ease
Until lava has sizzled
Everyone they knew
Involved in defying
The intensity of ***Hostility's Volcano***
Separated the sight of their bodies
From every watching eye imaginable

A Vague Account Of My Essence

As the murky morning fog clears
Who will be near
To witness
How to disassociate with the thought

Of me becoming deadweight
I choose to alleviate the grips of a disclosed fate
Relating to my new testament
Regarding having faith in

Ending the bewilderment among the dark clouds
Of the dark side
It's hard to hide from becoming desensitized
When the scope of oblivion

Shapes my *existence* and *family* origin
A cycle that keeps repeating itself
Where the curse of lost wealth
Has been passed down to inherited descendants

While the legacy of the aforementioned
Will remain intact
The fact that my identity has remained a mystery
After my obituary column was lost at sea ⇢

An accidental drowning on a cruise ship
Claimed my life unfortunately
While I was reading it
A Vague Account Of My Essence

Perceived a notion that was hard to believe
Truly indeed
My presence was too vague to see
From the very beginning

Endear To My Inner Being

Gaining strength daily
So I can venture through the land of the afflicted
My quest to connect with

The forces of the unseen
Gives meaning
For me to proceed with living a more fulfilled life

Clearing a path for a more profound vision
That will never betray
My true self in the end

Basking in the sun
Not in disarray yet I blend in like a chameleon
My presence is relevant only to those who embrace

Me without a clue
I now know why I'm here
The message is clear

Within my own personal virtues
It's free to choose where to spread your wings
In the end every lesson will be learned to
Embrace your new spiritual beginning

Healing Of A Wounded Heart

Feeling a heartbeat
That's been afflicted by tragedy
May remain wounded
Beyond disbelief
If the healing period

Has been prolonged
By the weight of resentment
For an occurrence
That starred as a catalyst
Named involuntary suffrage

For a greater good which has not yet materialized
Before the eyes of the afflicted partaker
Who's seeking shelter
Where *love* and *compassion*
Will volunteer to become a differential healer

Making the sufferer
A completely refined person
Once again
Where reassurance
To *trust* and *love* anyone

Became a special occurrence
When a wounded heart
Had a chance to be nurtured
For resurgence
To rejoin humanity's population

Of life's constant changing
Social orchestration
Deemed as fruition
Of a wounded heart forever strengthened
And never tender again

Truly Battle-Tested

No one else left to blame
When the chance came
To declare a truce
Over territory I've fought to claim
Who lost in vain?

A loser had to be eliminated
To make room for the winner
My *power* and *itinerary* was enough to uphold my rank
While defending my position on the battlefield
My tank broke down the competition

Plain and *Simple*
Fewer foes or *None left* will never rekindle
Their *desired* and *dictated* outcomes
For the causes I ***Truly*** embrace
While I've *sustained* and *endured*

The war
My flag of suffering is now waving in the wind
Because I have achieved a coveted position
By declaring myself the ***Battle-Tested*** champion
Forever a conqueror of any opposition that stands in my way

Manhood's Precipice

It's hard to be a man
In a land of desolation
People preying on others
You want to love someone else who is with another

It triggers
A sense of being vague
Within the shadows
Of what could have been

Time keeps ticking
Overpopulated twisted citizens
Contributing toward anarchy for personal gain
What's the *suffering* and *pain* going to lead up to

In the long run
It will all add up at some point in time
As I'm gazing at the social fabric of our world today
While staring downward at the edge of life's cliff

Picturing the landscape of daily corruption
I've realized paying attention is a must
For maximizing chances for gaining true *happiness* and *fortune*
During this one life to live ⇾

Can you understand the deeper meaning
Beyond your five senses
To relate to this passage
I've drafted for your eyes to see

As I said in the beginning
It's hard to be man
Of conviction within today's society
If you ask me

Conquering Disposition

I turn my back
On the nuisances in life
That impede my progress
Toward a more fulfilled existence
I've witnessed the vultures within the depths of darkness

Waiting patiently to feed off my success
As I'm taking a breath of fresh air
Out of the window of my fortress
Built from surviving tests
Disguised as conquests in the form of *duress* and *distress*

Imposed on the will of my true character
The barrier that has been lifted
Was a mirror image of what I truly had to fight for
What's now in store for me
Is to make it through the tunnel of reality

Tarnished by the scope of everyone's envy
So I can say in the end
That no one can emerge from the shadows
And take anything away from me
That I chose to accomplish during the race toward prosperity

Healed By Time & Redemption

The chance had come
To bear witness to the commencement
For honoring a prestigious literary talent
Everyone was waiting to hear his name
As the audience heard the speaker's introduction

It was a shame
He could not claim recognition for his achievement
Believing it was *a once-and-a-lifetime* predicament
Time had established an alibi
By creating a better fit crown

Disguised as an opportunity more *profound* and *endearing*
Than what was present regarding his first honorary ceremony
Clearly he was ecstatic by the *elements* and *events*
For redirecting the course of his destiny
The raindrops of redemption
Felt heavenly
As he read the invitation
To reclaim a lost yet newfound glory
He followed the instructions
Submitted his entry
And the rest was history
Healed By Time & Redemption
It's never too late to be claimed legendary
After the flair for your destiny was extinguished by calamity

New Poetic Kingdom By Reign

Where are the forerunners?
As I surpass them as a torchbearer
While illuminating my path toward stardom
Setbacks have *come* and *gone*
They've only made me stronger
As its cousin named misfortune
Tried to weaken my throne
I earned to be seated on
Yet my reign had not fell upon deaf ears
Whispers and *Cheers*
Well-wishers and *Peers*
Revere

My craft as a prolific poetic spokesman ringleader of
My kingdom includes the company of elite truth tellers
Who love to shed light on how you can enter
And become members of a newfound social class
Defined by me
A living legend who's not *an amateur* nor *a pretender*
I'm a winner by all means
I've come to be *published* and *awarded*
My *crown*, my *prize*, and *scepter*
As the new ordained ruler of a literary social class
Called the ***New Poetic Kingdom By Reign***

Unveil The Poetic Messenger

I'm glad
I'm just a visitor
Within a *socially desolate* land in disguise
How many more gimmicks
And clichés
Among the skeptics
Need to be mentioned
Just to pacify
My soul's inner cry for spiritual ascension
Attention has been given
To my physical shell

That I've dwelled within
For the time being
After acquiring the need to benefit
From broken promises
Mentioned
At the beginning of my upbringing
Made by the people I was closest to
Remains a clue
For the ages
As the pages of our lives
Are *on display* and *turned daily*

Unveiling why suffering is necessary
To understand
The hidden value
Of being human
Heightens the anticipated
And awaited reunion with our new paradise
It's in disguise as the eternal price
Which was paid for by this fleshly inherited treasure
The total measure of this fact remains true
Become a poetic advocate for change
To be considered a pure saint within this tarnished culture

A Transcending Social View

From dust to dust
I shall return
My vision to become whole again
Is a pure desire

To fix what's broken
Within my mental fixation
Is a token of my aspirations
To become a lifeline

For the honorable mentions
Who want to listen
While pleading for a sense of direction
In their lives

To pacify
The commotion
Concealed as a yearning for healing
Due to physical scars

That are
In front of my wayward eyes
Lies what they could become
Strengthening camaraderie

So the *social* and *economic* burdens
Within a land that's hurting
Are now a lightened load
To forebode an ethical way of living

Dissipating *malice* and *larceny*
The plea bargain for peace
Is now a new beginning
An option

They never knew it could've been chosen
Can now be explored
Because the higher self within themselves
Is not locked behind a closed door anymore

Desiring The Need For Advocacy

(Revised)

When people become broken
Unequivocally
The need for advocacy
To become whole as an individual
Resonates at its highest level

While wrestling spiritually
With preexisting conditions
The valley of needed seasonal changes
Needs to hear the cries
Of what's been seen behind

Watery eyes
Bearing with the discontented side
For what life has to offer
As *negative* and *incomprehensible* lessons
Are laid out along everyone's

Self-governed pathways
Subsequently our ancestry's destinies revealed
These blood-lined experiences
Ultimately *determine* and *shape*
Our earthly fate

Actively demonstrating
Why we're *currently* and *truthfully*
Seeking and ***Desiring The Need For Advocacy***
As were attempting to crown a declaration hierarchy
Dormantly dwelling within ourselves

Until the time when eternity's doors close *forever* and *ever*
Beyond our voluntary control
Located within the vicinity near
Life's perpetual circle of predestined concerns
For humanity as a whole

Cataleptic Ending

Needing to get out of this revolving door
Described as deceit
It's hard to explain the mystic
Of this gravitational force
Whose course of action
Has handcuffed my persona
Into a suppressed routine
Of daily mundane monotony

I want to express
The need for change
Yet my morale boosters stock has fallen
The evidence is shocking

As the value of it is worth nothing more
Than mere change within the loose pockets
Of my estranged memory
Happier times had clearly

Come about at one point in my life
What age range can I claim
To offset the vague strife
I endured
While being trapped within life's
Subliminal sabotaging revolving door
The sound of my gasping next breath
Will give me the strength

To break the whirlwind of dizziness
I've sustained
A new face will convey
A breakthrough conversation
Needing to take place during the foray
I can't erase this one fatal choice
Mistakenly claiming distress
As my own personal voice
I somehow used it for communicating the course
Of my deeds
Opening a self-sabotaging door
By force
A personal travesty
Brought on by me
Within my final hour of being
Human

Checkmated Adversity

My *Knight*
Has chosen to fight
In regard to my dreams
The suffering it takes
To materialize them
Raises the stakes
As my *Bishop* infiltrates
King Adversities *Pawn* gates.
Yet what awaited me was his *Queen*
Who always offers a challenging defense
To my conquering schemes
Setting up my trap
For a perpetual ending
A check was orchestrated by
My *Rook* to *King* Adversity
Followed by the capturing of his *Queen*
By my *Pawn* adding pressure
For a more profound ending
The final act was set for viewing
A checkmate
With my *Queen* cornering the *King's* throne
While my *Rook* and *Pawn* seized *King* Adversity.
My dreams have now been fulfilled
By defeating a formidable adversary
I chose to condone by contrary

Empowering Haiku

(Part 1)

Forget misery
I prefer prosperity
Ditch hypocrisy

Empowering Haiku

(Part 2)

Going for my dreams
Nothing's going to stop me
Destiny fulfilled

Finding Solace Within An Autumn Silence

(Version 2)

A calming cool wind
Makes its way
Through an open window
Welcoming a breathtaking scene

The unveiling of fluorescent-colored leaves
Marks a new seasonal beginning
Since our spirits
Are looking for comfort
From a nightly silhouette
Preceding the brisk overtones
Of a dawning sunrise

Our dearest desires
Are *hidden* and *embedded* within
The shadows of autumn's essence
Giving new *life* and *meaning*
To a wistful thought process
In the minds of weary lives

Who want to deaden the sounds
Of summer's extended daylight hours
More than ever
Most people strive
To obtain this soulful balance in life by
Finding Solace Within An Autumn Silence

The Next Loving Gardener

Men should treat women
Like lovely flowers needing
Tender *emotional care* and *showering affection*

Neglecting these fragile needs
Could turn your relationship
Into a lost perennial mystery

Leaving you all alone
Making you unable to become
The designated caretaker
Of every beauty seed
Dwelling within them
For all eyes to see

Representing a growing attractiveness
Forever bonding the essence
Of a *loving* and *mutual*
Relational chemistry
Between all *men* and *women*
Of humanity

Men be careful
In your own affectionate garden
Womanly rooted rose petals
Can always
Venture off and *Blossom* elsewhere
Ripping away the roots
Of any past candor gone wrong

Making way for a new
Courting cross-pollination
As they're on the move
To be in
The Next Loving Gardener's
Fertile and *Alluring* flower bed
Now seen as
A comfortable emotional abode
Once they've chosen to go down
Life's seasonal *potted* and *loving* road

A Season Of Chance

In the *Fall*
My chances to be lucrative
Indeed were numerous
Lotto numbers in sync
A jackpot within reach
Yet I was just one number off
To conquer all my worries

But in the *Winter*
A game of chance
Disguised as scratch-off
Helped me to advance
To only the bare minimum
Of winning five dollars
That was sort of depressing

So in the *Spring*
Why not visit Reno, Nevada
To see
If I could become a high roller
Overnight
But the whole weekend there was a bummer
Because the crap table
Became a gambling monster
Taking all my money
That was no fun either

So what the hell
I tried the Vegas Strip during the **_Summer_**
To make me feel better
As a failing gambler
Looking for more than just emotional comfort
I'm glad I made that move
Because my last dollar
Turned out to be good fortune
A ten percent portion of a million dollars
Was won playing the slots
Because the hot seat was given up
At the right moment
Indeed what a turn of events
To save my sinking gambling ship
So I could live the rest of my life
Happily extravagant

The Wrong Rose To Be Marrying

I don't why I chose to love her
Even though her allure
Attracted me to her sweet smelling deceit
As concrete as her first impression was with me
Gravity held down my expectations
As I held you in front of me
We were eye to eye

You were the color to my canvass
Your caress was soft as a fresh red tulip
At last you were pure enough
To be lucid for a cherished experience
Of what my heart had wished for
I hope you will be willing to endure
The *trials* and *tribulations*

Of all the future loving exposures my life has in store for you
Yet our adventure to together
Will not remain after sunrise has imposed my free will
To *resist* to *exist* with you as a valued commitment
Will now become a thrill for the ages
As the vague pages to the new chapters
Of our estranged courtship

Will not become an Oscar Award–winning script
I will never have to tell a lie
To build up the privacy fence needed to protect me
From your evil eye you imposed duplicity to
Release your sweet-smelling lovesick toxins
As we lived our lives *daily* and *relatively* close together
We lay beneath the presence of your *sweet lips* and *velvet touch*

Will always remain a temptation at its best
When the sun sets
I'm having no regrets
As to why
We were once *man* and *wife*
You were the poison to my ivy
That's why I had to cut you out of my life

Seasons Of Change

In the ***Fall***
I learned to crawl
As I came into the world
A beginner
So when the following ***Winter***
Approached
I was in awe of what I could become
Within society's reality
Then in the ***Spring***
I *grew* a little *taller* and *began listening*
To *ways* and *trends* of the living
While peeking in through the door
Of infinite opportunities
So maybe later
I could spread my wings
Fly away and *Eventually become* somebody
But then finally ***Summer*** decided
To *show itself* and *reign supreme*
Because the chance to become illustrious
Had perfect timing

Poem #25

(Unifying The Poetic Collection Titles)

Being Alone In A World Full Of People (Version 2) #1
Sparked
The Waiting Game #2
Because I was *Disgusted From Within #3*
Due to being stuck in
Hostility's Volcano #4
As the drama unfolded
A Vague Account Of My Essence #5
Had been *Endear To My Inner Being #6*
So the *Healing Of A Wounded Heart #7*
Preceded being *Truly Battle-Tested #8*
Was the basis for my *Manhood's Precipice #9*,
Which strengthened the *Conquering Disposition #10* within myself
I was *Healed By Time & Redemption #11*
To solidify my *New Poetic Kingdom By Reign #12*
Then I had been able to *Unveil The Poetic Messenger #13*
So he could share *A Transcending Social View #14*
Desiring The Need For Advocacy (Revised) #15
Regarding my *Cataleptic Ending #16*
I *Checkmated Adversity #17*
By using my *Empowering Haikus (Parts 1 and 2) #18–#19*
This inspired *Finding Solace Within An
Autumn Silence (Version 2) #20* ⇗

I submitted a copy of ***The Next Loving Gardener #21***
To a professional female editor
During ***A Season Of Chance #22***
That attracted me to ***The Wrong Rose To Be Marrying #23***
Only to recognize that during ***Seasons Of Change #24***
Poem #25 became the **twenty-fifth** installment
For this poetic masterpiece which remains
Forever seen as a leading trademark of an edifice
Later adding notoriety that would benefit my enduring legend

Renaissance Poetry Writing

A way with words
Observed by a critiquing
High-esteem nobility
Changing the literary forefront
By the brunt of a dying past time
Indelibly reviving a genre

Into a new-wave era
After reforming conformed minds
Into joining
An iconic calligraphy movement
Now deemed as
Renaissance Poetry Writing

The Various Shades & Textures Of Humanity

We've all seen this kaleidoscope
Showcasing every ethnic image
As one before
Yet we're still
Naive to the allure
For inclined cultural diversity

Savoring an educated perspective
After advocating
A unified cultural distinction
Lies in a fight against ethnic extinction
A motion toward
Promoting longevity survival techniques

So every race
Can maintain their own ethic specialties
Ranging from *food* and *language* to
Style of dress and *Even physical distinctive traits*
Authenticate and *Represent*
The Various Shades & Textures Of Humanity

If every ethnicity
Were blended into one being
It would be
A Beautiful Godly Image
For all to see within its finished entirety
Like a treasured painting
On display within a famous art museum's
Gallery of masterpieces

The Value Of Friends

It's a special type of connection
For wherever you go
Familiar faces show
Memorable festive occasions
Within the memory of the sole observer
Known as the mingling initiator
Cherishing *each* and *every* associative partner
That's universal across

All *borders* and *time zones*
Reinforcing one common link
As they're a foundation for
This kindred association of personal bonds
We suppose will remain
Up *close* and *personal*
As long as the people
You're truly looking for

Are right under
Your *nose* and around the *corner*
Waiting to expose
Their real value as forever friends
Who embody similar true virtues as you
The initial guardian of sociability
Will be displaying
Each and *Every* friendship

Now being comprised
On a written wall mural
For all *to see* and *have a clue*
In relations to who you are as
A person of noteworthy social influence
Tried and *True* as a fine wine with
An appreciative acquired taste
From a wine taster praising yet

Toasting to ***The Value Of Friends***
"Salud Or Cheers To"
Who will be there for you
No matter what outcomes life decides to dictate
For *now* and *forever*
Your friendship's future keepsakes
Are *possible* and *obtainable*
As you reach your peak within societies treasured social hierarchy

Living Life & Loving The Thrill Of It

It's the best experience
Known to humanity
Living Life
Bears portentous fruit
During our youthful days
As adolescents we progress
More and *More*

As adults we grow
Along the worldly racetrack
Of pretentiousness
Bearing with all *present facts* and *potential setbacks*
Spurs us into
Loving The Thrill Of It
Yet how can we only have

One entire lifetime spin on our destinies
Regardless of gender
It's a rare hindrance
Where time is the only formality
Controlling the speed
Of our individualized experiences
So I guess as a witness

Of this permanent contingency
It's plain as day to see
Living Life & Loving The Thrill Of It
Within its entirety
Will forever be
Our greatest gift during *each* and *every*
Prestigious season within our inevitable reach

Poem #30

(Inquisitive Fame Acquisition)

Who holds the key to my salvation
Even though my deeds
Have marred my path toward
Inquisitive speculation by many

The relationship between *notoriety* and *pacifying*
The need for popularity
Acquisition
Is diagnosed as publicity
A drug that exposes the extent of hidden ulterior motives

Showcased by the host of the media frenzy
To support this theory
Monetary greed is
Subdued by financial clarity

Clearly erasing any shadow of doubt
As to who I am
Still remains the best mystery to figure out
As I'm walking within society

Handling and Minding my own business quietly
I have no need to shout out my purpose for being
Why expose my identity
Alleviating the pressure to feed into
A fabricated image of
Fame
The masses have now decided to cater to
When you're truly somebody
The world revolves around you

If You Could Go Back In Time (What Would You Change?)

(Part 1)

Rewinding the clock
Back to a past time
Exactly during your prime
Where everything you ever wanted
Was within reach
As realty was teaching you
An unforgettable lesson

In the final say for
(What Would You Change?)
That can't be undone
Would it be that lost love
Who got away
Where cold feet intervened in the worst way
Ending an anticipated engagement

Was it really meant to be
To some *extent* or *degree*
What about cashing in
On a pivotal moment
In your personal history
Where the real lifestyle
You would've been

Living today
Was a heartbeat away
Back in the day
Yet you missed that chance
By forever closing
Your life's book of
Proposed prosperity pages

If You Could Go Back In Time
(What Would You Change?)

(Part 2)

During your lifespan
Those pages where read aloud
After reality's present-day edits
Were credited
Following the last act
Of your recorded soul's

Exact utterances'
Seen and *Heard* by all
Was the demand for
Your past heart's desired fortunes
Encrypted within a message
Translated by your future self

Standing behind a subjective podium
While illustrating on a remedial stage
Why so many *woulda, coulda, shouldas*
Are in abundance as we age
If You Could Go Back In Time
(What Would You Change?)

A Deadening Cycle Of Relived Dramatizations

How long
Has it been
Since a chosen
Breakthrough appeared
To be free from
Our *repetitive* and *shackled*

Frame of mind
Who never really knew
It clearly grew
Into a reality
Without key illustrations
Of gleeful moments

Pictured as smiling faces
Branded with self-resolve
Had now evolved
Into an illusive
Immunity token
Thrown toward

Our crying altar's
Peaceful call
For a changing chance
At ending
Our personal lives' saga from
A Deadening Cycle Of Relived Dramatizations

Dying Just To Live Again

(The (I) Version)

Making it to the grandstands
Of eternity
Is a reminder that we're only here
For the sake of
Dying Just To Live Again

There's a spin on this metamorphosis
Like seeing the sight
Of a caterpillar turning into a butterfly
So it can experience
A greater peace while flying in sky

Freely
Never ever being subjected to scrutiny
Of any kind
Is a true reminder as to why
Our civil duties within our lifetime

Need to be fulfilled
Before the final day of preparation
Sponsored by free will
Regarding our exit date
Merits the fact that

Before going on display
In the midst of fellow
Friends and *Brethren*
Whose lives were influenced by our presence
Have come to pay their last respects

With class
While partaking in
A universal blessed aspect
Deemed as a short-term
Living privilege

Everyone has called
You've touched my life
Now I'm saying goodbye
As I'm cherishing the fact that I'll be
Dying Just To Live Again
So *I* too can join my dearly departed friend
One day once again in the serenity
Of the afterlife

Yesterday's Ghost Town

Our *thoughts* and *decisions*
Have led us to a place
Where the foggy mist
Of our past
Has taken ownership

Of a realm
We would only dare
To be a part of
If life worked out
The way we planned

The debut of this trailer
Within our minds
Showcases every
Fantasized portrayal of
A cliché called

Reality's Showdown At High Noon
It's a forging gun battle
With *Us* versus *Dreamful Death*
Previewing the end result
Of our mystic future

This visual premonition
Will forever draw attention
To every forgotten aspect
Of our destined daily lives
Only If

We lose to
Dreamful Death
We'll ultimately
Become one with
Yesterday's emerging ***Ghost Town***

Venturing Down This Unknown Road

It's that dreaded feeling
When you've taken
A wrong turn into believing
You're almost there

Even though being
In the middle of nowhere
Is reason enough to contemplate
A low gas gauge

Is now on *E*
Bad *mapping* and *timing*
Are enough to cause despair
Within the mind of a nervous driver

Whose unquestionably sure
He's hit a dead end
Not reaching his true destination
While being lost

Within a thick fog of endless speculation
Which will never *clear* and *unfold*
Your destination after regretfully
Venturing Down This Unknown Road

The Darkened Whirlpool

Humanities funneled
Social downfall
Had spiraled
Empathetical dreams

Into an unknown realm
Of calmed deceit
Where menial minds
Could only survive off

Curiosity alone
With nothing left of themselves
For their own souls to condone
The cycle of ambiguity

Forever *drained* and *postponed*
Any acts of positivity
During the daylight hours of
The Darkened Whirlpool

Delirium

Too much to lose
With not enough time
To gain
What's rightfully important

Is sanity's *profane* and *grave* influences
Will push the envelope
For what needs to be
Commencing imaginatively

Reality displays psychotherapy
As the elements
Of a mental disturbance
Truly matter

Within the cellar
Of our inner mind's corridor
Is gravity's wane grip
On psychic deviancy

Heard *loudly* and *subconsciously*
Is the turning
Of a psychological doorknob
Opening a mental squeaking door

Labeled
Beware Of A Unseen Disturbed Forum
Within a psychical realm
Called ***Delirium***

The Tale Of A Restless Heart

Weariness has made
A restless heart
Feeling relentless
To absolve
The wrongs of all loved ones
Who've been involved

With hardships
Beyond their control
The blood of self-sacrifice
Keeps this heart pumping
To help fulfill
A morally uplifting

Devoted family obligation
From the start
By contrast
It's a relative's redeeming art
That's showcasing
The Tale Of A Restless Heart

Moments Of Peace

A calm wind
Before a treacherous storm

Sitting in a lounge chair
Within a screened porch

By the same token
Meditation behind closed doors

Resonates a sanctity like
Walking along the ocean shores
Of contentment beach
By far
These *Moments Of Peace*
Speak for themselves with ease

Wanting To Love Who We Can't Have

Across a room
In a social setting
You see someone
You want to love in life
Then *lo* and *behold*
A flirtatious situation unfolds
You see her
She sees you
Or in most cases
She sees you first
Then you notice what's possible
In your love life
As the glare for
The trading places stare
In the eyes of both parties
Remains strong as the attraction
For love at first sight
Then the plight of reality shifts to
Unveil her *husband* and *immediate family*

Sitting together at your favorite restaurant
A clouded vision
Now has both hopefuls emotionally distraught
Over how their
Commitment and *Relationship* timing were off
Not favoring each other
For this present-day fantasy
At hand
Which will never come true
While being in view of
A love you'll never have
During this pretentious moment
Of a deeming chance
For flirtatious affection
Gone in an instantaneous
Waving of realities hands
Only to acknowledge friendliness
Remains an unnerving saving grace
Against confrontation for ***Wanting To Love Who We Can't Have***

Getting Lost Within The Gaze Of Your Lover's Eyes

It's an enchanting
Display of devotion
Seen through love's
Gripping hold on
Your loving emotional state
As the sight
Of *your lover's eyes*
Perpetuates what it's like
To feel *sought after* and *truly treasured*
In a sense
Where time momentarily stops

And coupled sensuality
Will only last for a brief eternity
As two infatuated heartbeats
Are heard alike
After riding a passionate
Merry-go-around
Of a loving chemistry
Sparking an alluring element
For what it genuinely feels like
To be desired after
Getting Lost Within The Gaze Of Your Lover's Eyes

A Written Picture Of Our Desired Portrait

(A Poetic Narrative)

A fresh take on
Our unified vision
Here is my written line
Added as a contribution
In order to redefine
Our blank canvas
I am awaiting your written brushstrokes
In order to complete
What has already ingeniously commenced

As I sit, holding this paintless brush
In a room filled with shadow
My situational serenade longs for color
Hues of black and white
Beautiful in their simplicity
I anticipate your lines and verses,
As a winter tree waits quietly
For the coming of spring

Falling from this poetic tree
Are those spring leaves
Fluorescent and *Chromatic*
Resonating a *harmonious* and *joyful*
Penned collaboration unveiling
"A Written Picture Of Our Desired Portrait" ⤳

Together creation is inevitable
A dawning of intricate devices
That breathe life into dusty delusions
Where life is ripe with intense scarlet
Ochre and Sapphire skies
Painted with two hands and yet
Coming together as one

How fortunate is it
To discover an opportunity
For embracing an artful
Poetic alliance
While anticipating written brushstrokes
Giving *new life* and *meaning*
To our penned overture in the making

Embracing Love's Forgotten Companion

(Original Vows)

Love was taking a journey
With two heartbeats
Uniting as one
In harmony with symbolic
Holy matrimony
Regarding a potentially blissful
Horse carriage ride
With each other
"Reading Just Married"
Remained the hopeful
Vision of the bride to be
As it coincided with
The groom's infatuation for his fiancée's
Deep-seated adoring beauty
Within her inner heart's locket
While yearning for her beloved
To find the key
Unlocking a romantic door
Hidden within the purity of her complexion
Almost fulfilling his obligation
In relation to their future wedding destiny
While being tenderheartedly soft-spoken →

So he could be committed to her forever
As the aura of her vanity
Sparked a lasting ***devotion***,
Which had yet to be
Embraced as *Love's Forgotten Companion*
This vital part of their loving chemistry
Would be needed
In order for the groom's "***I do***"
To eliminate his cold feet issue
As the ceremony commenced
That fateful moment
Happened in an instant
He looked at her
She looked at him
He was frozen
As he stared at the priest
Then again to her with ease
He said, "***I do***,"
Remembering in the back of his mind
He had to kiss his bride
While ***Embracing Love's Forgotten Companion***
Now became his constant ***devotion***
Toward his *new* and *lovely* wife

Embracing Love's Forgotten Companion

(Renewed Vows)

Walking down the aisle
Of holy matrimony
With **devotion** for the aura
Of her vanity on his mind

The *groom* and his *adorning bride*
Accompanied love
On a journey to find
A forgotten companion

Embracing and *Finding* commitment
As *time* and *infatuation* drew them together
In favor of their union
Were wedding guests in awe of this endearing pact

Sitting in their pews looking at
Who would be involved in
Such a pivotal decision
Tried and *True*

Embracing Love's Forgotten Companion
Gave everyone a preview of hope
For partaking in lifelong vows
Drawing a man closer to his wife →

Solidifying the reason why
This sacred partnership
Will set an example
On how to live a more *fulfilling* and *prosperous* married life

The Loving Mystery Man

(A Secret Admirer's Perspective)

(Reprised)

He loves being incognito
Like a secret admirer with bravado
Intrigued by her profound beauty on the go
He gazes at her stilettos
She's as lovely as a *Japanese Lotus Blossom* in bloom
Mysteriously he assumes
That one day out of the blue

She'll finally have a clue
As to *when* and *who*
Her secret admirer will be as his sweet gestures
Will finally be in plain view
Exposing his true virtues
For trying to daringly pursue
The depths of her *soul* and *womanly figure*

Admiring Her & Her Heart From Afar

I was in awe
Of her beautiful skin
As the beating of her heart
Radiated a sense of compassion
I pursued my treasured infatuation

Every time I glanced at her
Breathtaking figure
Each second remained worthwhile
Forever in a moment seeing
The apple of my eye

For the time being
I became a heartfelt
Admirer from Afar
I only dreamt about
Her loving gestures of tenderness

Toward me
As I was inconspicuously noticing
Her making eye contact
With me gingerly as
I hoped to make

An initial first impression upon
My *one* and *only* adorned
Womanly work of art
By capturing her golden heart
Of mesmerizing beauty

Her Undeniable & Admired Presence

The sight of *her* nakedness
Healed and *Cleansed*
The loving hearts of most men
In more ways than one
They'd never imagine
It'd only happen

Once in a lifetime
Where *her* figured appeal
Remained worthy
Throughout *her* time
Monogamy had momentously birthed
A committed art form

Where cordial minds
Devoted to relational men
Hoped a portrayal of genuine courtship
Could certainly exist
One day as
Her Undeniable & Admired Presence

The Alluring & Disenchanted Black Widow

Her hourglass figure
Had caught my attention
A *keen* and *enticing* infatuation fueled
A ravenous need to be
A part of a *perspiring* and *thrill-seeking*
Wicked desire
Has set the stage

For a daring
Face to *Face* encounter
With a beloved caterer
Serving up this fatal attraction
As a deadly poisonous
Scent of decadence
Worth flirting with

Until her gratification process
Reaches a level of triteness
With her lover
Held at bay
Be aware of
Her seductive spell
Every admirer ➴

May not live to tell
About escaping
A fateful dying ending
Lurking within her mind
As her intentions were open like a nightly window
Defining her as
The Alluring & Disenchanted Black Widow

Admiring Her From Afar

I was in awe
Of *Her* beautiful skin
As the soft texture of it
Radiated an accompanied
Vibrant hairstyle
Along with a gorgeous smile
I had to stare inconspicuously
Every time
I glanced at her
Breathtaking figure

Every second remained worthwhile
As I was seeing
The apple of my eye
For the time being
It may have seemed like
I only dreamt about
Witnessing and *Embracing*
The glare within those eyes
Of mesmerizing beauty
She became my contagious →

New valentine
As I became a heartfelt
Admirer From Afar
Forever noticing
My vivacious queen to be
As time marched on
I hoped to make
An initial first impression upon
My *one* and *only*
Adorned female work of living art

Drifting Into The Winds Of What Could Be In Life

Drifting emotionally
Into the Winds
Of What Could Be In Life
Jet streams of formalities
Blowing constantly
Take forms of
An enlightenment wind
A prosperous wind
A devastation wind
A destiny wind
A conspiracy wind
A sinful wind

Blowing social winds
Swept away
All of the populaces
Demand
For being intuitive
With the origins
For why the occurrences
Of these drifting social winds
Have come to pass for
Making an impact
Changing and *Shaping*
The populaces exact →

Future outlook on life
In light of today's yesterdays
While anticipating
What's yet to come
In the midst of
Yearning for better days
Lying within
The next drifting surge
Of omnipresent
Daily social winds
Being held at bay
For What Could Be In Life

Poem #80

(Setting Sail For A Poetic Voyage)

Being the captain
Of eighty individually named poetic vessels
Has been a rewarding experience
Destined for departure
At the stroke of an undetermined hour

Getting ready to endure this literary tidal wave
Meant to *empower* and *not persuade* critics
To become indifferent
Regarding the ripple effect
For this distinctive written vision

Partaking in a voyage
Where ***Inner Distinction***
Is ***Socially Feasible***
For ***Life (A Burden or A Privilege)***
Where ***Cherished Breaths***

Will be needed to establish a ***Cured Precariousness***
As I'm destined to reach the shoreline of an ***Ocean Bliss***
At the end of this poetic voyage
Will be the formulation of ***A Calming Breeze Of Serenity***
That will carry on this legacy at hand

Poem #90

(Breaking New Ground For What's Yet To Come)

Throughout the backdrop
Of a socialized canvas
Stands an intriguing figure
Who's having a chance
To win an internal battle of emotional chess
The purpose for this
Remains key

For setting up his own morale
Universal decorative standard
While vowing to empower
And promote a need for
Positive social consciousness
Because the greatest test of all
Will be the focus needed for

Getting over set hurdles
Within life's uncertainty
Obstacle course for promoting
Blinding pitfalls
Of *regret* and *remorse*
Set up to strengthen one's character
Will falter by the waste side

Because reaching ***Poem #90***
Will set the tide
As it's coming in
For illuminating my poetic dreams shoreline
Of the masterpiece possibilities
That have yet to be written
In the present time of B-poet's prime

Poem #100

(Setting The Stage For *A Poetic Visionary*)

As the curtain rises
All eyes are on
A Poetic Visionary
Standing
Behind a golden podium

All ears
Are bound to hear
This coveted message of poetic diction
In relation to the words
Setting The Stage For

An illustrious overture
Of cascading works
From *past, present,* and *future*
Foretelling
Spoken *eloquently* and *endearing*

Leaving the crowd in awe
Wanting more of what's yet to come
An anticipation of new material
Yet to *unfold* and be *heard*
Before the *ears* and *eyes* of captivated audiences

Was evident
For pouring out his soul
Was needed
After he finished
His current spoken masterpiece

Before the final act
Yet a last curtain call
Had to fall
Causing a *cause* to *cease* poetic mastery
Remained a true mystery

Until this poetic visionary has reached
Poem #300 may become
The final written masterpiece
At the end point of
A long poetic visionary journey

Poem #500

(One Quarter Of A Poetic Pinnacle Completed Vision)

A symbolized **Poem #**
Strikes a chord
To be remembered
From afar
As a **500** yard

Written landscape
Captivates
A thirsting taste for
One Quarter Of
A Poetic Pinnacle vineyard's

Wisdom grapes
Are daringly hung from vast vines
Ripe with wined diction
Each poured glass of
A reader's convictions

Are brought to life
After moving indulgence's
Are sought after
By one's eyes
A respectful truth

Further lies
In a renewed wholeness
Seated deeply within themselves
As a reasoned
Self-prophesied *Completed Vision*

AUTHOR'S PROFILE
B-POET

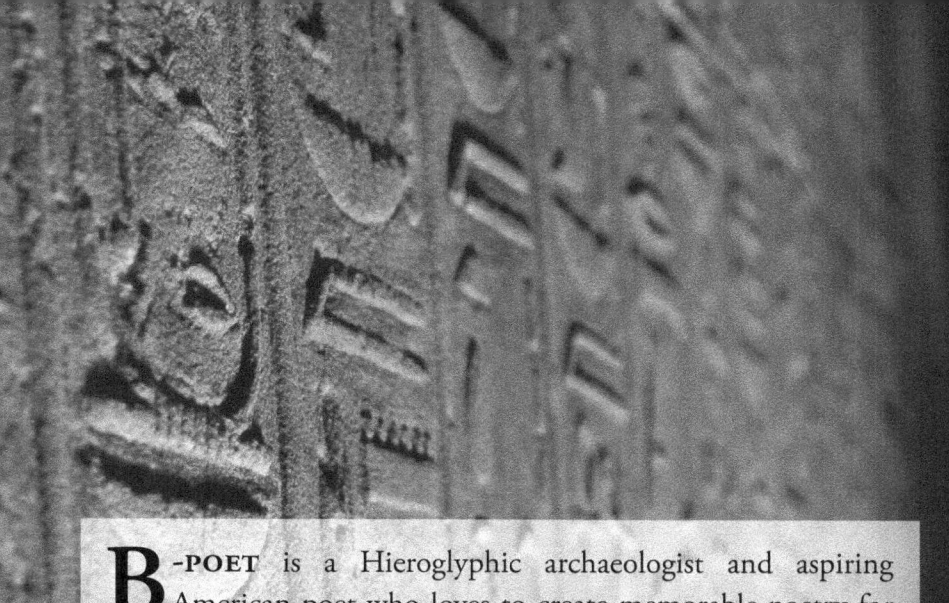

B-**POET** is a Hieroglyphic archaeologist and aspiring American poet who loves to create memorable poetry for every adoring fan who loves to appreciate the written art of written self-expression. He originates from Indianapolis, Indiana; His passion for poetry and writing remains to be a prime catalyst for his own poetic expertise. His poetry has been showcased internationally as BK in a poetry book titled *International Who's Who of Poetry 2012*. His poetry has also been featured as BK in the United States as well by Eber & Wein Publishing which includes these poetry compilation books: *American Poet, From A Window: Wistful Thoughts, Best Poets of 2014-2016,* and *Who's Who in American Poetry 2016-2017*. His hobbies include reading, writing, listening to music and traveling. He can also be followed on twitter at www.twitter.com/newfacepoet.